PHENOMENAL MOMENTS

REVEALING THE HIDDEN SCIENCE AROUND US

by science photographer

Felice Frankel

CONTENTS

INTRODUCTION

AS A SCIENCE PHOTOGRAPHER and research scientist at the Massachusetts Institute of Technology, I capture images of research in various labs. Many of the photographs are used for research publications, visually showing the science. Sometimes the images appear on journal covers, which helps bring attention to the research. Every day I am introduced to various scientific phenomena, and because of that, I see connections to the world around us. That's what this book is about.

Phenomenal Moments started years ago when cameras in phones became good enough to create high-quality images. Like most people, if I have my phone in my pocket, I am more apt to take pictures as I go about my daily life. Recently, I realized I had accumulated a significant collection of images that could tell the story of how science is all around us. In my job as a scientific photographer, I usually use my Nikon D850 DSLR "real" camera with a 105mm macro lens. Sometimes I put the camera on a microscope, but recently, I have been using my phone, especially for the images you will see in this book. The phone is a quick way

I have the best job in the world. I am constantly learning about science because of the pictures I take. As an example of what I do, I've included an image I took of a material called ferrofluid. Ferrofluid is a suspension of very small pieces of iron in oil. I placed a large drop of the material onto a glass slide. Under the glass slide is a yellow sticky note, and under the yellow sticky note are seven circular magnets. You are seeing the iron particles responding to the magnetic fields made by the magnets. If you look carefully, you can see the pane of the window I used to light the setup. You can also see the green card I held over it to reflect a little color. And if you look even more closely, you can see the lens of my camera. Not something I meant to happen!

of capturing phenomena when I have to get the shot at that moment. The technology still has its limitations, but it gets better every year.

The most important difference between my real DSLR camera and the phone is the image quality, in terms of the file size. File size is the amount of digital information you capture. The more information you capture, the more you see and the clearer the image is when you enlarge it. Phone cameras are getting better with file size, but they still don't compare to DSLR cameras. However, there is nothing more convenient than a phone camera. I don't carry my Nikon with me all the time because it is heavy and I usually have to use a tripod with it. While most of the images I made for this book were taken with the phone, a few were captured with the DSLR and a couple were made with a flatbed scanner. It's amazing what you can create with a scanner. Scanners also vary in the quality of image they can capture. A scanner that allows you to set the dots per inch (dpi) is the best for high-quality images.

The book is organized into five sections that explore light and shadow, form, traces left behind, transformations, and surfaces. Each section opens with an image that demonstrates the theme of the chapter. After the opener are a number of double-page spreads, each with a section of a photograph that serves as a kind of window

of the complete image you will see when you flip the page. It's like a guessing game. Try to guess what the larger image is from the section that is initially shown. Each full-size image is accompanied by a description of how I made the image or a personal anecdote, noted as a "moment." This is followed by the "phenomenon," which is a description of the science involved in what you see. The last spread in each section has a pair of images sharing a similar phenomenon. My hope is that you will remember these images as you go about your daily life. You will understand what you are seeing and maybe be inspired to take your own pictures.

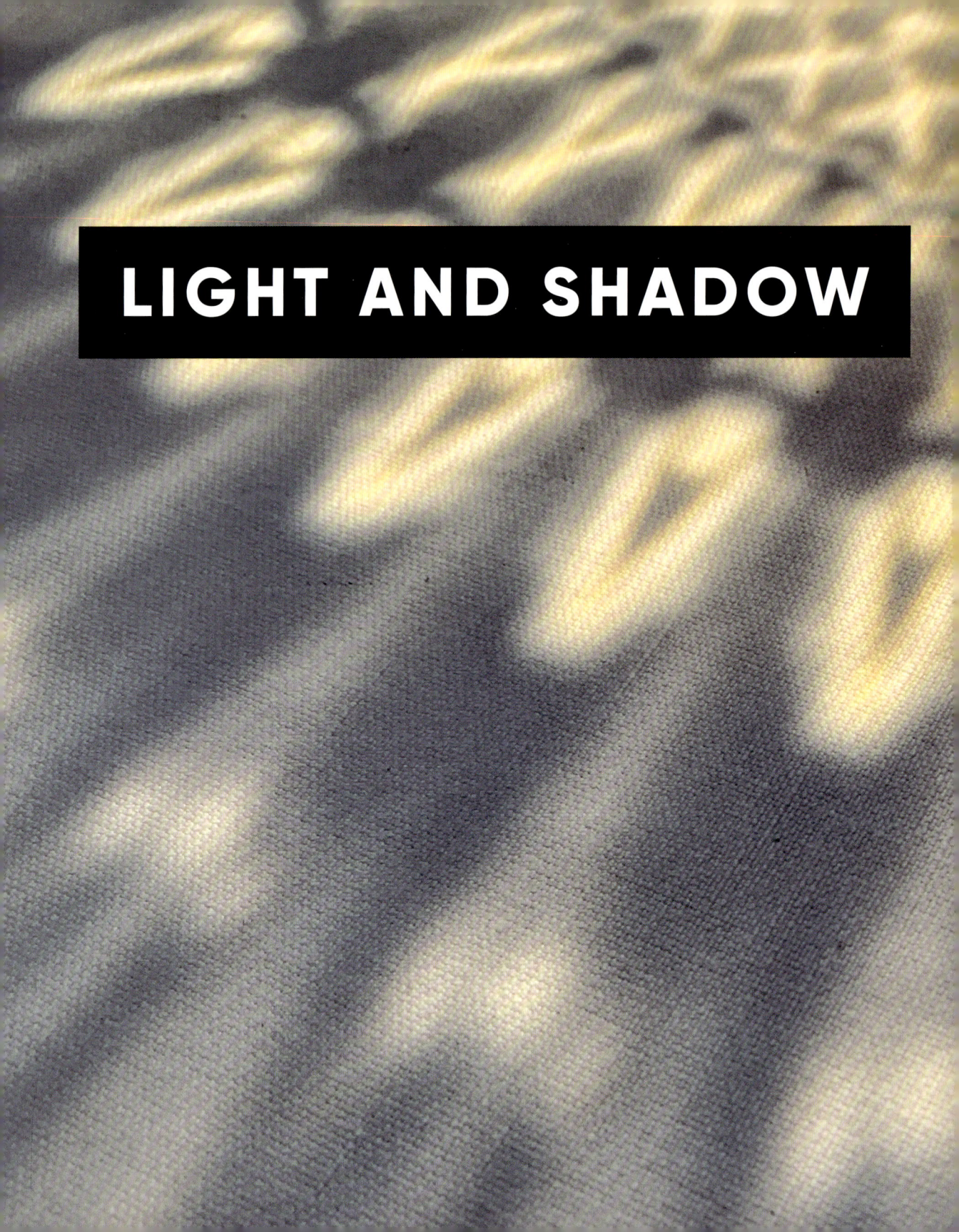

LIGHT AND SHADOW

WHAT DO YOU SEE?

MOMENT I was playing around one day and placed a few almost transparent pieces of fabric with similar weaves over one another and saw the surprising phenomenon of the overlapping fabric. I quickly went to find my DSLR camera. At the time, I was not using my phone to take pictures since the quality of my phone's camera wasn't quite where I wanted it to be.

PHENOMENON The overlapping fabrics create **moiré patterns** (*moiré* is the French word for "watered"), referring to an old technique for making textile patterns. The fabric used to make moiré patterns was traditionally silk that showed a rippled, or "watered," appearance. Two layers of silk fabric with similar spacing in the weave were dampened and pressed together. Slightly shifting one layer at an angle to the other created the pattern, which remained after the fabric dried. Researchers are able to produce similar patterns using graphene sheets. Graphene is a two-dimensional material consisting of a single layer of carbon atoms arranged in a hexagonal lattice. When one sheet overlays the other, moiré patterns are formed.

WHAT DO YOU SEE?

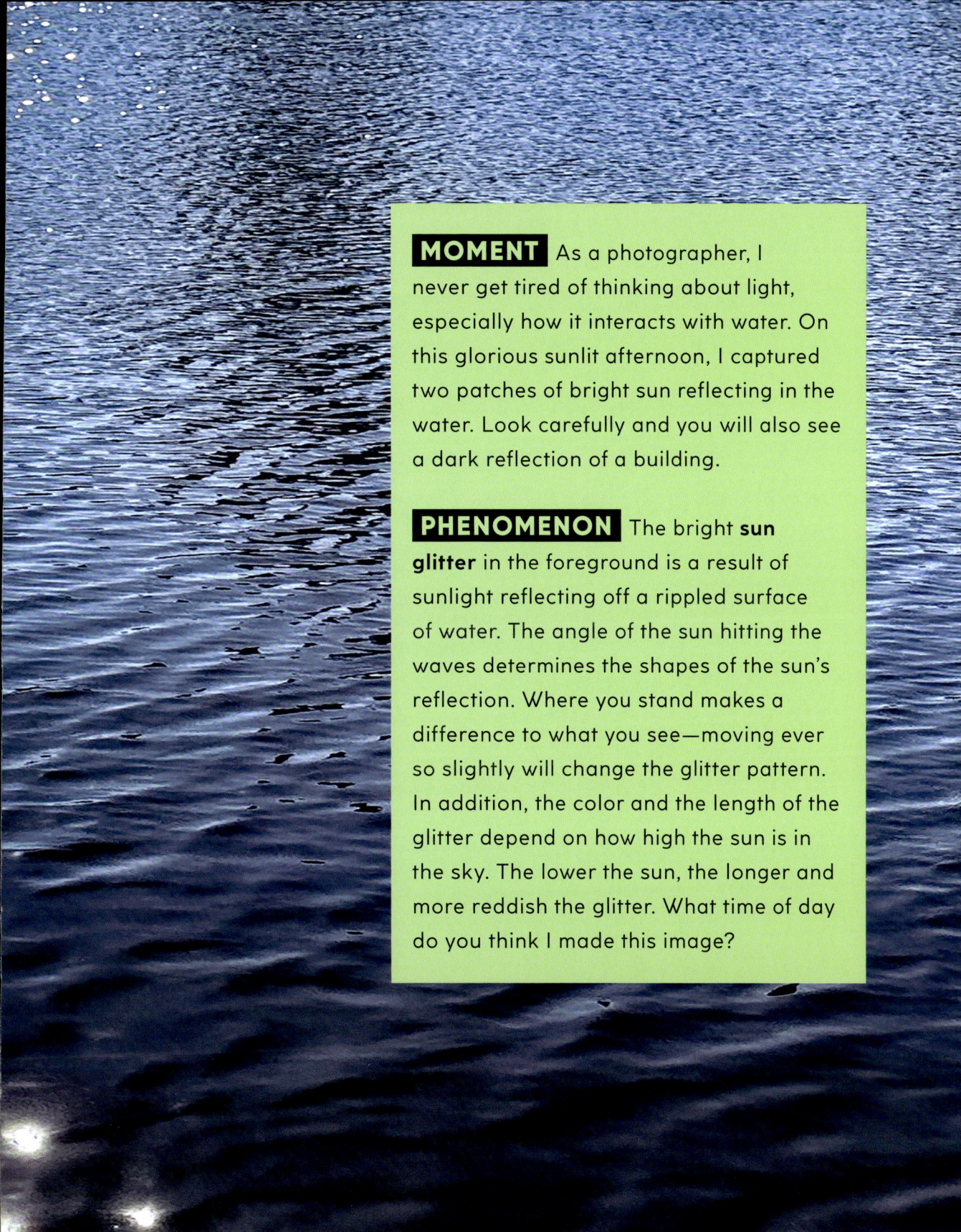

MOMENT As a photographer, I never get tired of thinking about light, especially how it interacts with water. On this glorious sunlit afternoon, I captured two patches of bright sun reflecting in the water. Look carefully and you will also see a dark reflection of a building.

PHENOMENON The bright **sun glitter** in the foreground is a result of sunlight reflecting off a rippled surface of water. The angle of the sun hitting the waves determines the shapes of the sun's reflection. Where you stand makes a difference to what you see—moving ever so slightly will change the glitter pattern. In addition, the color and the length of the glitter depend on how high the sun is in the sky. The lower the sun, the longer and more reddish the glitter. What time of day do you think I made this image?

WHAT DO YOU SEE?

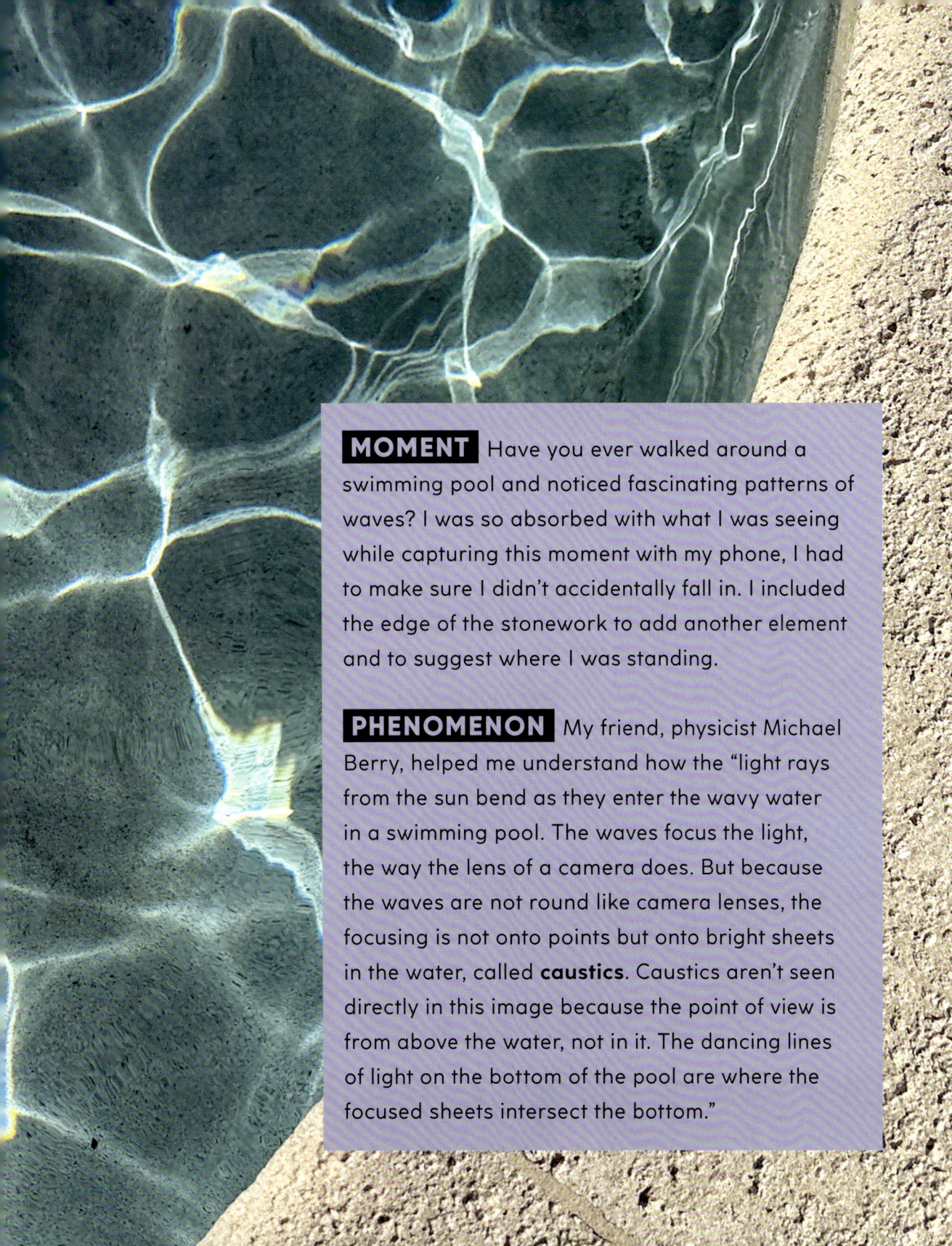

MOMENT Have you ever walked around a swimming pool and noticed fascinating patterns of waves? I was so absorbed with what I was seeing while capturing this moment with my phone, I had to make sure I didn't accidentally fall in. I included the edge of the stonework to add another element and to suggest where I was standing.

PHENOMENON My friend, physicist Michael Berry, helped me understand how the "light rays from the sun bend as they enter the wavy water in a swimming pool. The waves focus the light, the way the lens of a camera does. But because the waves are not round like camera lenses, the focusing is not onto points but onto bright sheets in the water, called **caustics**. Caustics aren't seen directly in this image because the point of view is from above the water, not in it. The dancing lines of light on the bottom of the pool are where the focused sheets intersect the bottom."

WHAT DO YOU SEE?

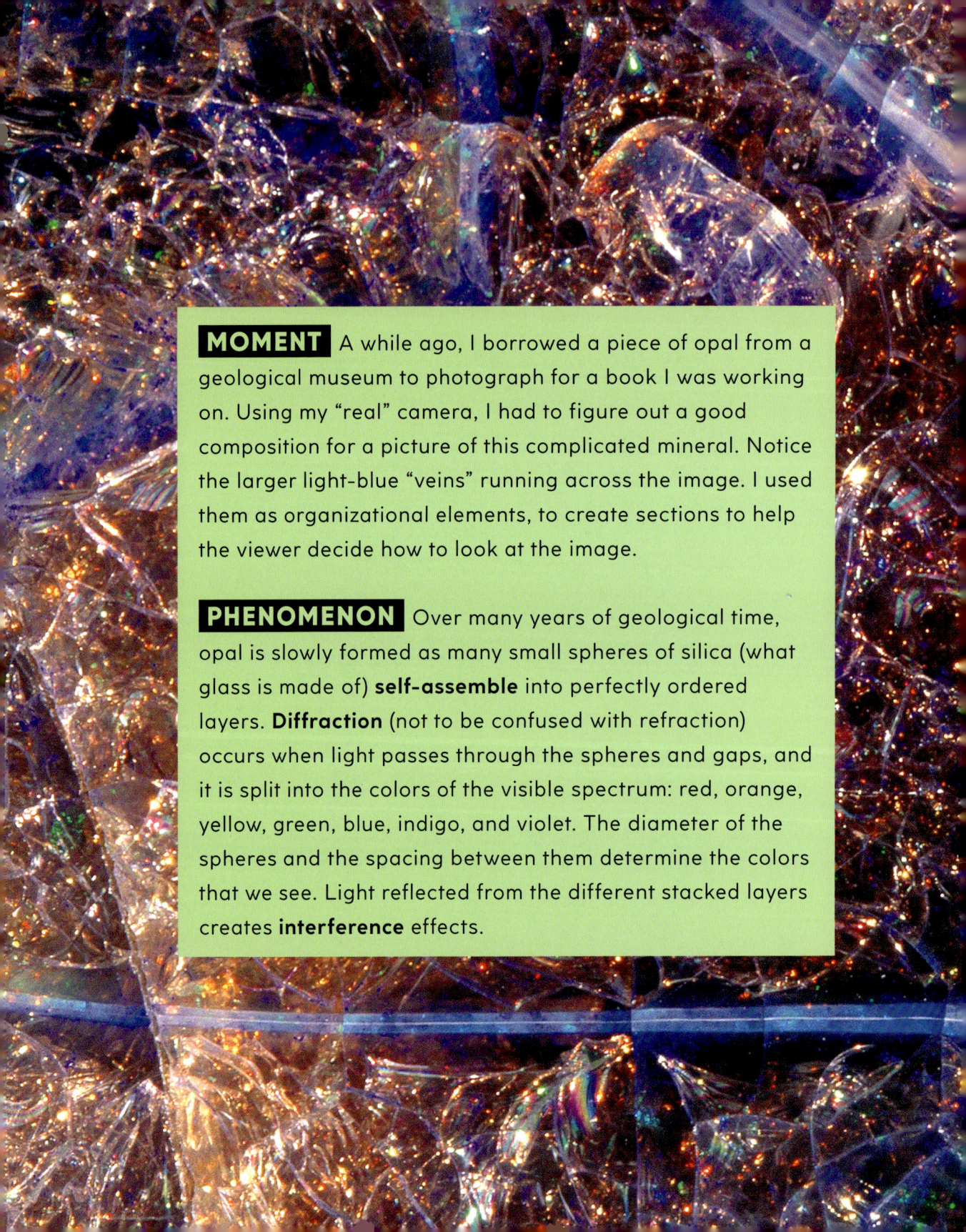

MOMENT A while ago, I borrowed a piece of opal from a geological museum to photograph for a book I was working on. Using my "real" camera, I had to figure out a good composition for a picture of this complicated mineral. Notice the larger light-blue "veins" running across the image. I used them as organizational elements, to create sections to help the viewer decide how to look at the image.

PHENOMENON Over many years of geological time, opal is slowly formed as many small spheres of silica (what glass is made of) **self-assemble** into perfectly ordered layers. **Diffraction** (not to be confused with refraction) occurs when light passes through the spheres and gaps, and it is split into the colors of the visible spectrum: red, orange, yellow, green, blue, indigo, and violet. The diameter of the spheres and the spacing between them determine the colors that we see. Light reflected from the different stacked layers creates **interference** effects.

WHAT DO YOU SEE?

MOMENT Here is another image I made with my real camera for a book. My coauthor and I decided to use a simple drop of water to explain how molecules form in a water drop. In this case, the drop is falling from the end of a syringe. Can you imagine how many pictures I took to get just the "right" drop?

PHENOMENON A drop of water can sometimes act as an **optical lens**. The drop brings into focus the light from what is behind it, an ordered array of an artist's watercolors. My friend Phil Ball reminded me, "This is exactly what Antoni van Leeuwenhoek relied on to make his microscopes: he made the spherical single lenses from droplets of hot glass, which he then polished up a little." Van Leeuwenhoek is known for his pioneering work in microscopy in the seventeenth century and was the first to see microbes.

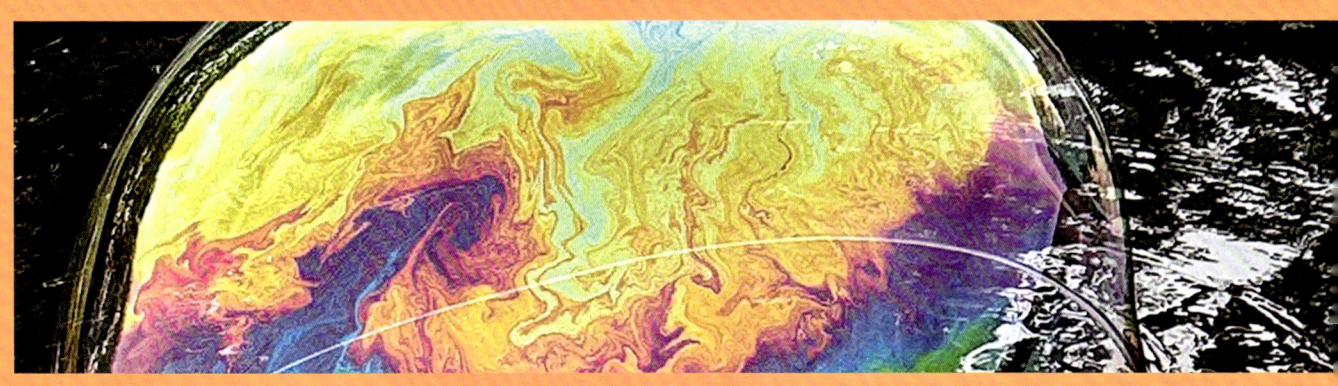

WHAT DO YOU SEE?

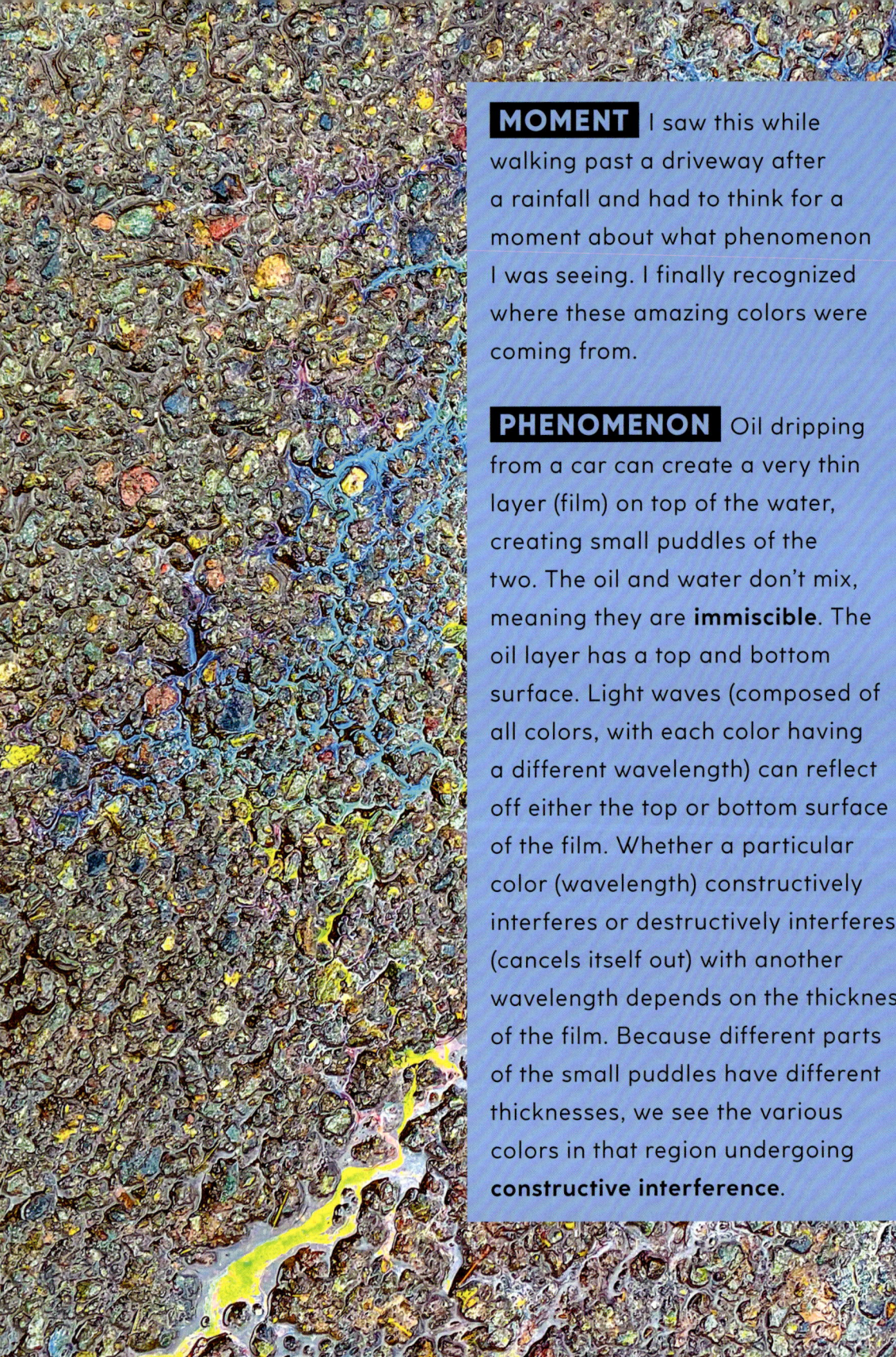

MOMENT I saw this while walking past a driveway after a rainfall and had to think for a moment about what phenomenon I was seeing. I finally recognized where these amazing colors were coming from.

PHENOMENON Oil dripping from a car can create a very thin layer (film) on top of the water, creating small puddles of the two. The oil and water don't mix, meaning they are **immiscible**. The oil layer has a top and bottom surface. Light waves (composed of all colors, with each color having a different wavelength) can reflect off either the top or bottom surface of the film. Whether a particular color (wavelength) constructively interferes or destructively interferes (cancels itself out) with another wavelength depends on the thickness of the film. Because different parts of the small puddles have different thicknesses, we see the various colors in that region undergoing **constructive interference**.

MOMENT In the spring, the "bubble guy" gathers his huge metal circle, dips it in a soap solution, and carefully moves it through the air to produce these enormous bubbles. I was able to use my phone to get a quick shot of a bubble before it burst.

PHENOMENON Giant bubbles also show **interference** effects caused by light reflecting from the inner and outer surfaces of the soap film. In addition, because the thickness of the film changes across a gradient on the bubble's surface, we see an array of beautiful swirling patterns. This is called the **Marangoni effect**.

FORM

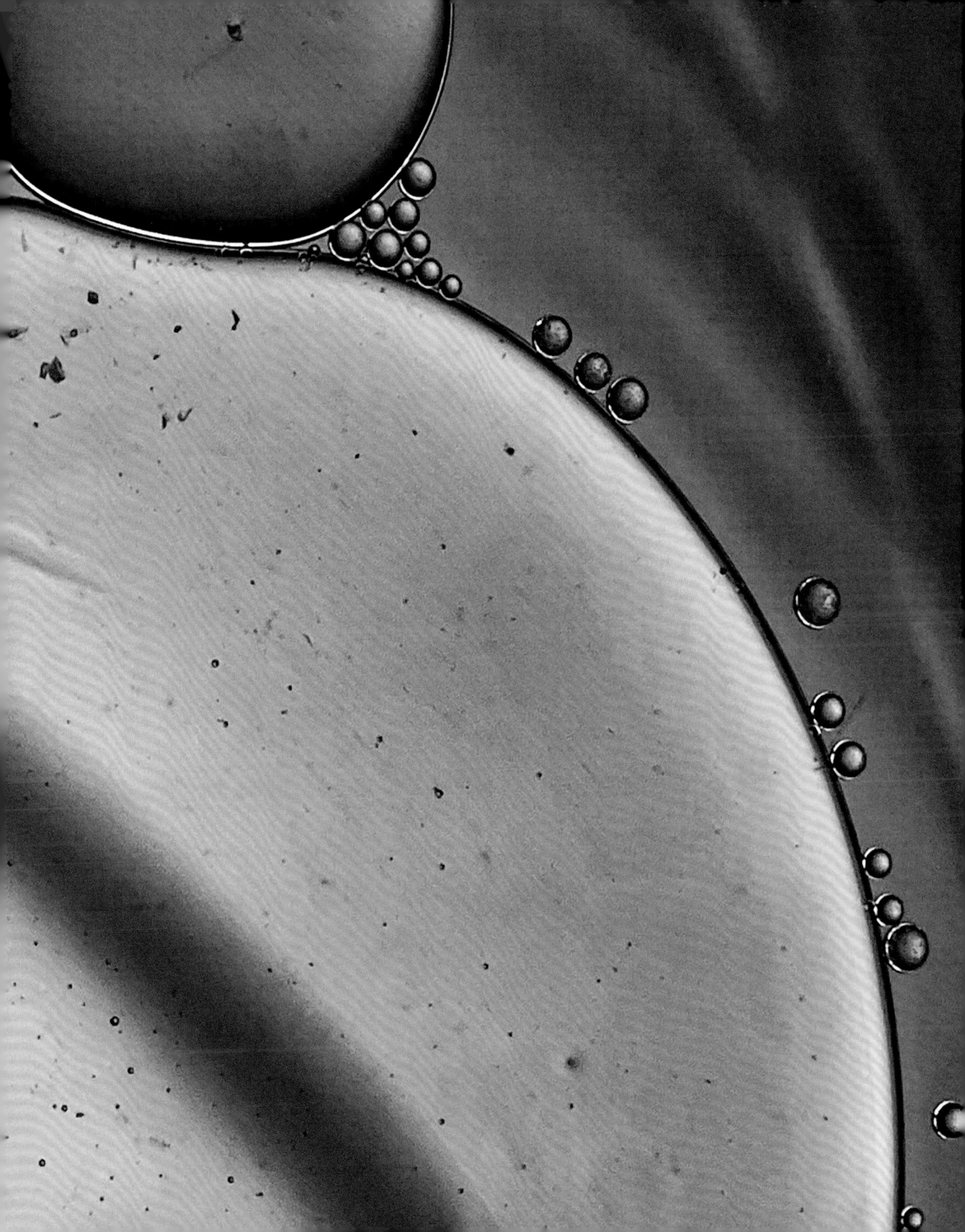

WHAT DO YOU SEE?

MOMENT While shopping in the produce department, I found these weird-looking strawberries. Well, I thought that's what they were, but I was mistaken. I had to buy a few to photograph them and study them further.

PHENOMENON Have you ever seen white strawberries? It turns out that they are not strawberries but pineberries, which are very similar to the red strawberry we are used to seeing. When you bite into either white or red, you will notice there are no seeds inside. That's your hint that, surprisingly, neither of these berries is technically a fruit. By definition, a fruit is a plant's ripened ovary, containing seeds inside, like an apple or an avocado. Yes, an avocado is a fruit! Both of these types of berries appear to have "seeds" on the surface, but those dots are not actually seeds. They are the plant's ovaries, called **achenes**. Pineberries and strawberries are classified as multiple fruit because each one of their achenes is a separate developed fruit with a seed inside.

WHAT DO YOU SEE?

MOMENT I was sitting on a stoop in New York City and was immediately taken by a transparent shape that glistened as I moved my head back and forth. I picked it up and studied it and was surprised to discover that it was a wing of a dragonfly. I found a few others and decided to carefully put them in my wallet. Luckily, they lasted the train ride back home to Boston. I made this image with my phone attached to my magnifying microscope.

PHENOMENON The amazing network of patterns on dragonfly wings is a result of their wing **venation**, which refers to the arrangement of veins, cells, and supporting structures throughout the wing membrane. Each wing displays a distinct pattern, similar to our fingerprints. At first, I thought I was seeing a similarity to a honeycomb structure, with a regular pattern of polygons, but I was wrong. The dragonfly wing's overall boundaries, important in making the wings aerodynamically efficient, determine the shape of patterns.

WHAT DO YOU SEE?

MOMENT One thing I continue thinking about is that every image I make can always be better. Always. I question if I could change the composition or improve the focus. Sometimes it is difficult to figure out exactly what will make the image better. I loved the subject of this image when I made it, but my phone didn't give me the clarity I wanted. For this book I reshot the image with a newer phone that gives a larger file size, which resulted in a clearer image.

PHENOMENON After blowing bubbles into a glass dish of coffee using a pipette (a hollow glass tube used like a straw to move liquid), I observed the bubbles first making contact with each other and then "bursting" to form larger ones, a process called **coalescence**. A similar phenomenon happens to form rain—smaller droplets coalesce in clouds to form raindrops.

WHAT DO YOU SEE?

MOMENT Some of my friends brought me a handful of flowers one evening. I remembered from taking a botany class that a certain type of flower, like a daisy, is considered to be a "**composite**" in the family called Compositae. This gerbera is one example. To make this picture, I lay the flower flat on my flatbed scanner and set the resolution high so that I would see the amazing details.

PHENOMENON Although it appears to be a single stunningly beautiful flower, the gerbera is a composite of hundreds of flowers with three different subgroups. The central disk, appearing green here, contains the subgroup called disk florets. Surrounding the central disk are the trans florets. Look carefully in the trans area to find the small yellow structures. These are **stamens**, the male organs responsible for producing pollen. The outermost subgroup, pinkish here, consists of the ray florets. It's pretty amazing if you think about it—that each small flower within the large flower is genetically programmed to develop a particular form.

WHAT DO YOU SEE?

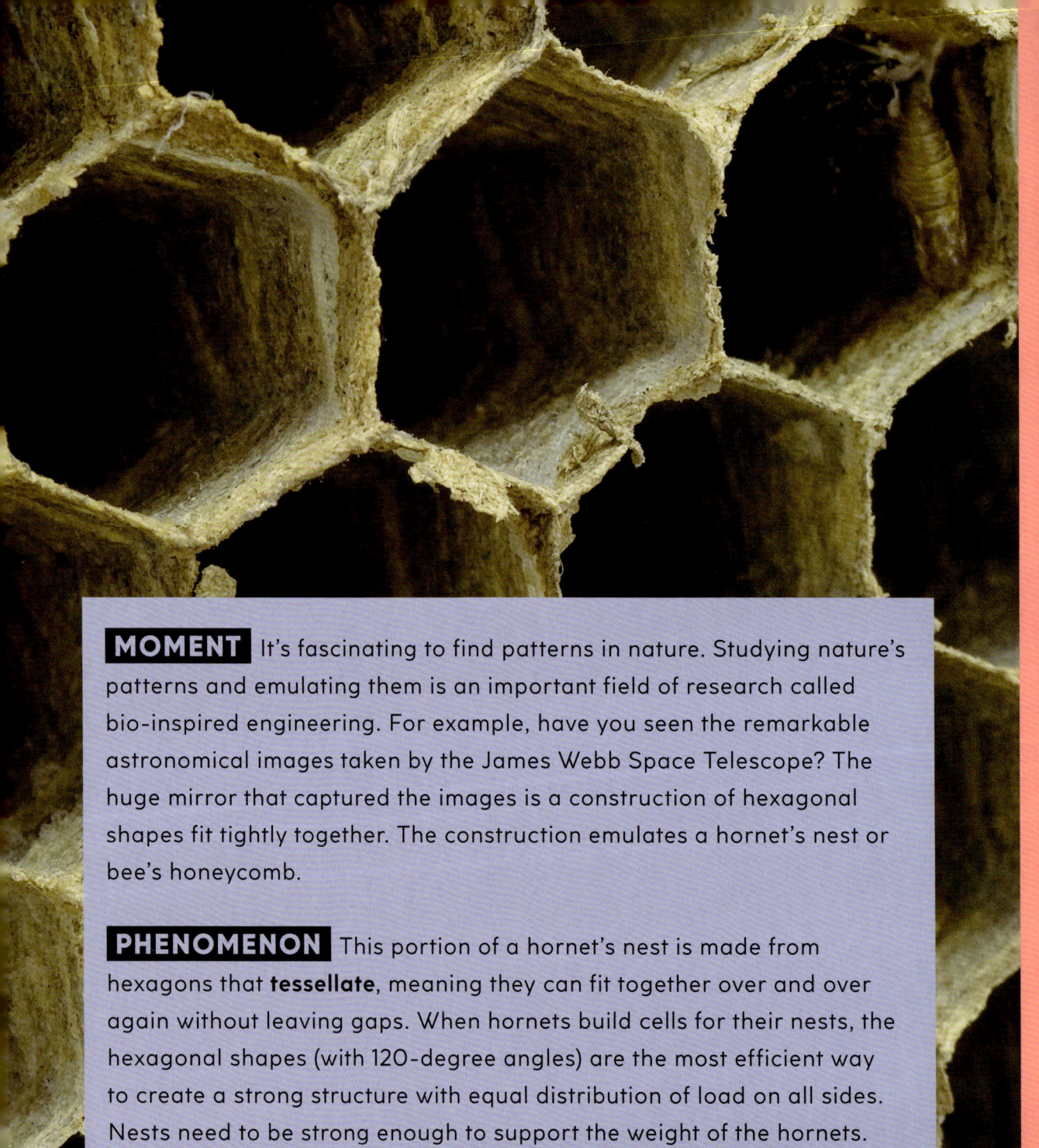

MOMENT It's fascinating to find patterns in nature. Studying nature's patterns and emulating them is an important field of research called bio-inspired engineering. For example, have you seen the remarkable astronomical images taken by the James Webb Space Telescope? The huge mirror that captured the images is a construction of hexagonal shapes fit tightly together. The construction emulates a hornet's nest or bee's honeycomb.

PHENOMENON This portion of a hornet's nest is made from hexagons that **tessellate**, meaning they can fit together over and over again without leaving gaps. When hornets build cells for their nests, the hexagonal shapes (with 120-degree angles) are the most efficient way to create a strong structure with equal distribution of load on all sides. Nests need to be strong enough to support the weight of the hornets. See if you can find a remnant of a hornet in the photo.

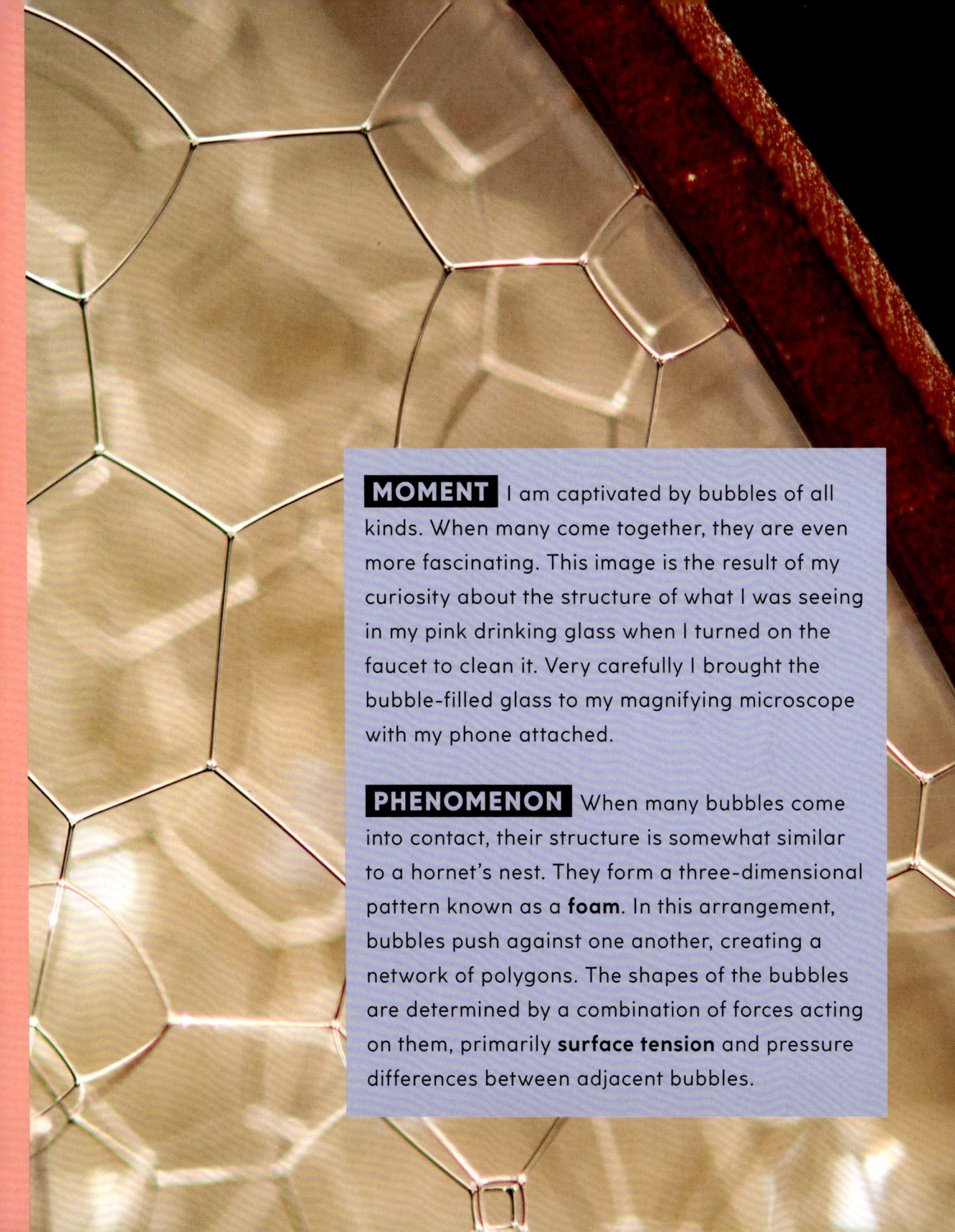

MOMENT I am captivated by bubbles of all kinds. When many come together, they are even more fascinating. This image is the result of my curiosity about the structure of what I was seeing in my pink drinking glass when I turned on the faucet to clean it. Very carefully I brought the bubble-filled glass to my magnifying microscope with my phone attached.

PHENOMENON When many bubbles come into contact, their structure is somewhat similar to a hornet's nest. They form a three-dimensional pattern known as a **foam**. In this arrangement, bubbles push against one another, creating a network of polygons. The shapes of the bubbles are determined by a combination of forces acting on them, primarily **surface tension** and pressure differences between adjacent bubbles.

TRACES

WHAT DO YOU SEE?

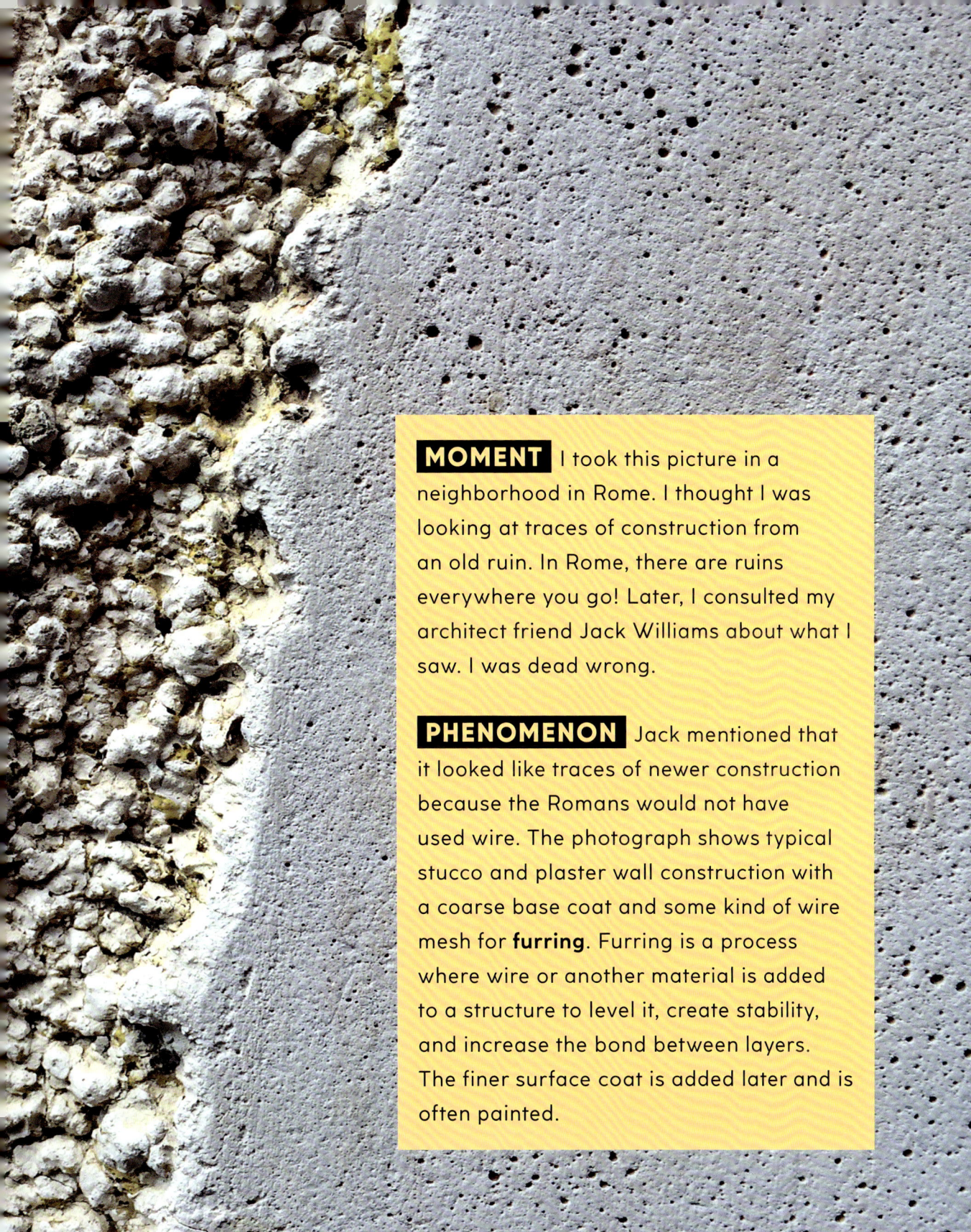

MOMENT I took this picture in a neighborhood in Rome. I thought I was looking at traces of construction from an old ruin. In Rome, there are ruins everywhere you go! Later, I consulted my architect friend Jack Williams about what I saw. I was dead wrong.

PHENOMENON Jack mentioned that it looked like traces of newer construction because the Romans would not have used wire. The photograph shows typical stucco and plaster wall construction with a coarse base coat and some kind of wire mesh for **furring**. Furring is a process where wire or another material is added to a structure to level it, create stability, and increase the bond between layers. The finer surface coat is added later and is often painted.

WHAT DO YOU SEE?

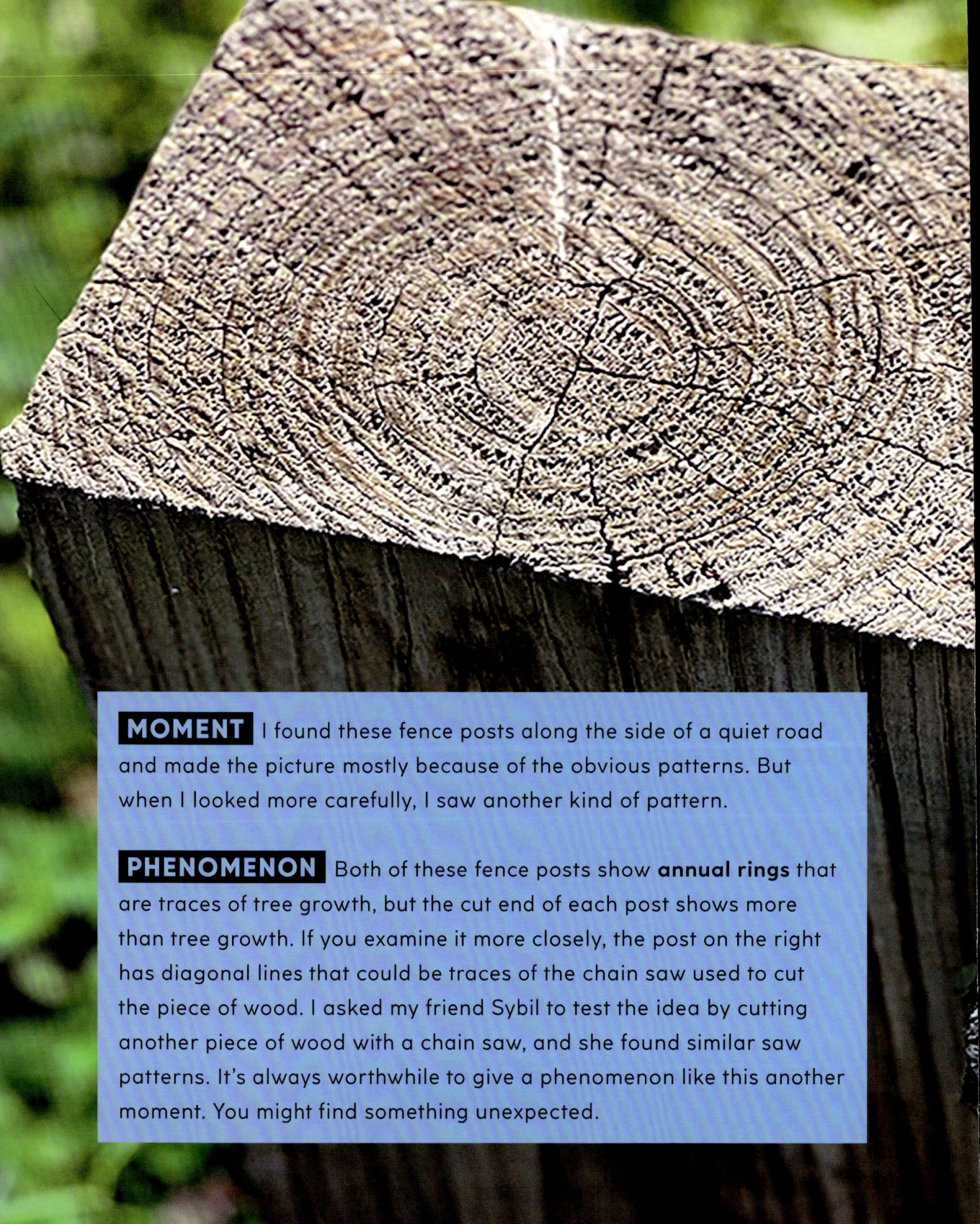

MOMENT I found these fence posts along the side of a quiet road and made the picture mostly because of the obvious patterns. But when I looked more carefully, I saw another kind of pattern.

PHENOMENON Both of these fence posts show **annual rings** that are traces of tree growth, but the cut end of each post shows more than tree growth. If you examine it more closely, the post on the right has diagonal lines that could be traces of the chain saw used to cut the piece of wood. I asked my friend Sybil to test the idea by cutting another piece of wood with a chain saw, and she found similar saw patterns. It's always worthwhile to give a phenomenon like this another moment. You might find something unexpected.

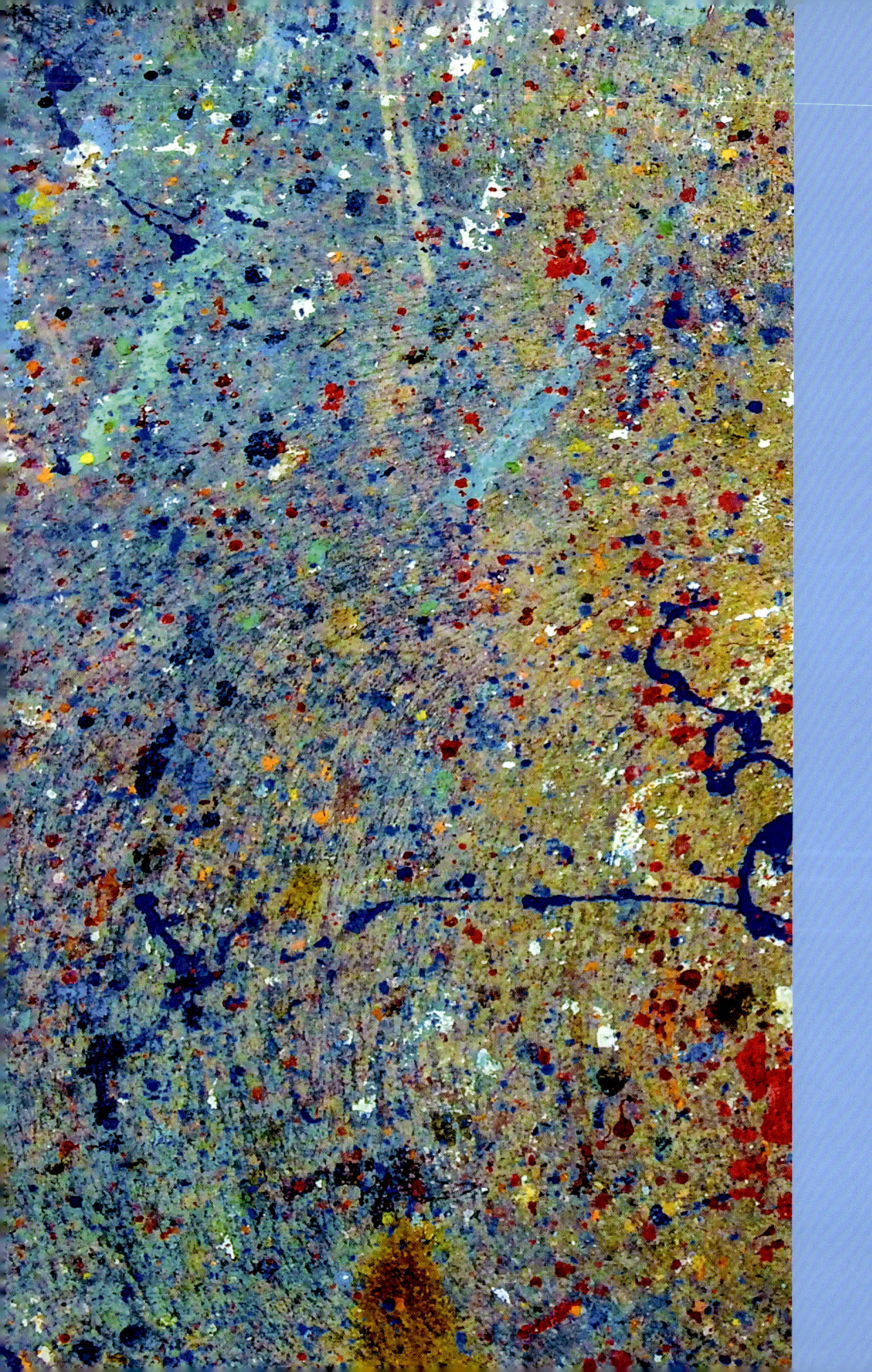

WHAT DO YOU SEE?

MOMENT While walking past a storefront that was being painted with all sorts of colors, I noticed quite a bit of the paint splattered on the sidewalk. It reminded me of a Jackson Pollock painting. He intentionally used a splatter technique on his canvases. I am not sure what the storefront painter's intentions were.

PHENOMENON The patterns of droplets, dribbles, and swaths of paint depend on the **viscosity**, or the thickness, of the paint and its **surface tension**, or the force that holds the molecules of a liquid together. Other factors, like surface texture and weather conditions, also affect the outcome. Want to try it? If you do, please make sure you cover the floor with paper!

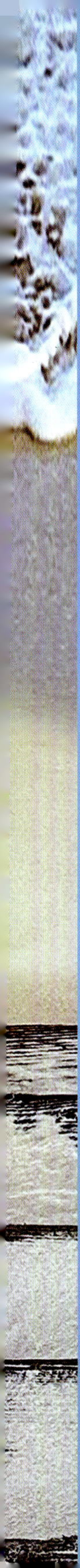

WHAT DO YOU SEE?

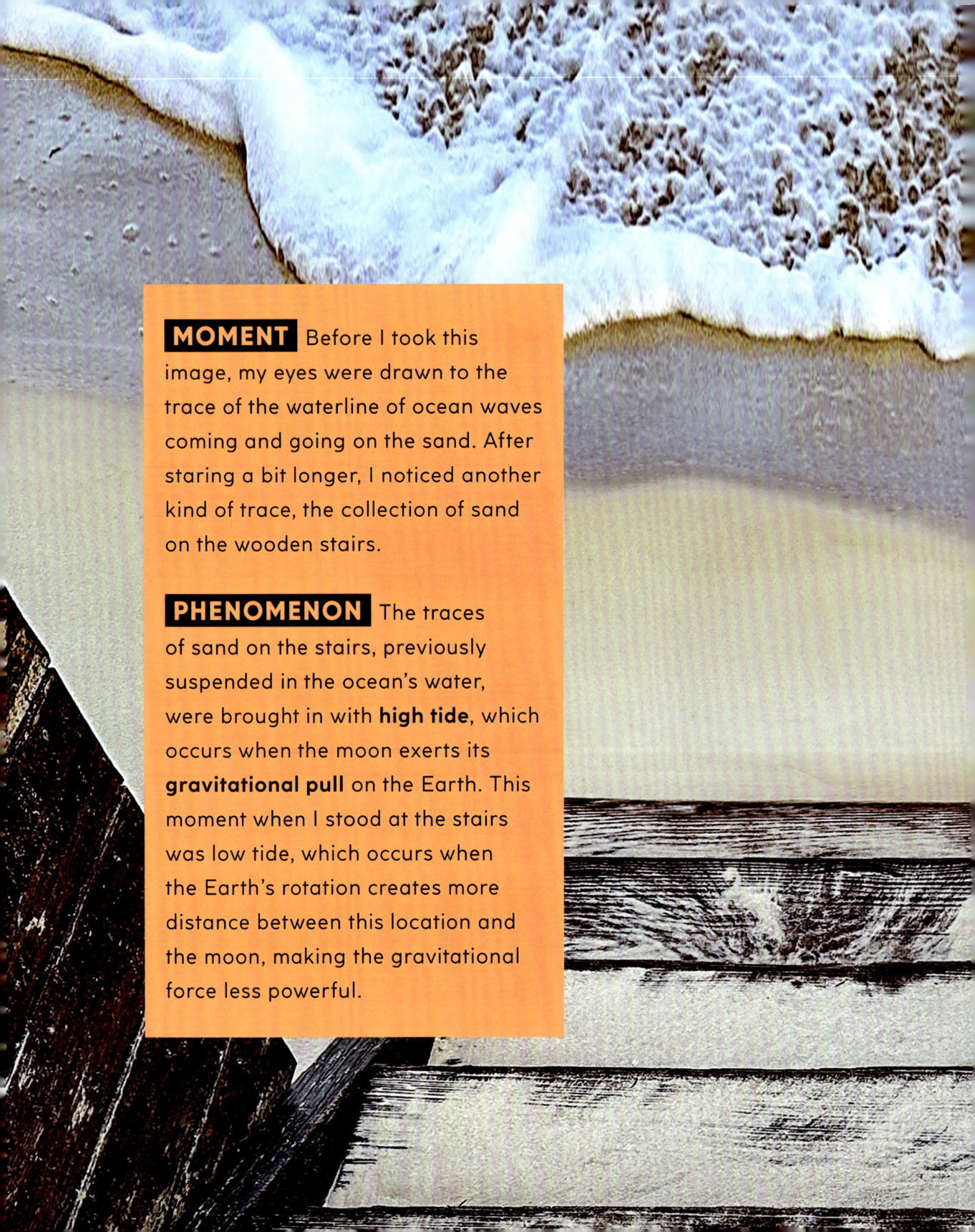

MOMENT Before I took this image, my eyes were drawn to the trace of the waterline of ocean waves coming and going on the sand. After staring a bit longer, I noticed another kind of trace, the collection of sand on the wooden stairs.

PHENOMENON The traces of sand on the stairs, previously suspended in the ocean's water, were brought in with **high tide**, which occurs when the moon exerts its **gravitational pull** on the Earth. This moment when I stood at the stairs was low tide, which occurs when the Earth's rotation creates more distance between this location and the moon, making the gravitational force less powerful.

WHAT DO YOU SEE?

MOMENT Here again, I made these two images far apart in time. I realized later that both were showing a similar phenomenon. For the first, do you see anything a little weird about the mud footprints?

PHENOMENON The pattern in the mud involves **deformation mechanics**. When force is applied to the mud, it responds, resulting in footprints. They were, of course, not part of a planned design, but they create patterns nonetheless. If you look carefully, you will see that they were not made by the same type of shoe.

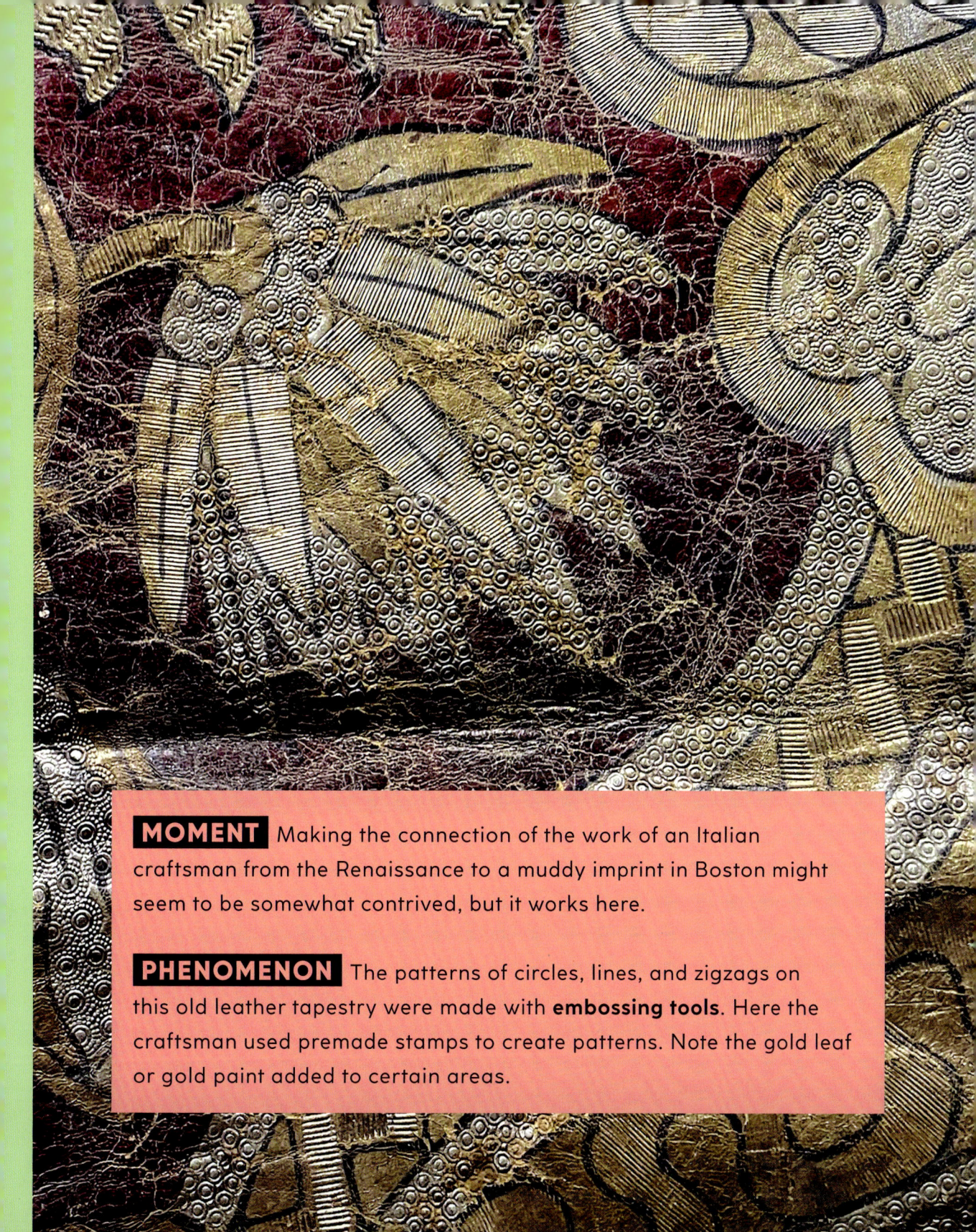

MOMENT Making the connection of the work of an Italian craftsman from the Renaissance to a muddy imprint in Boston might seem to be somewhat contrived, but it works here.

PHENOMENON The patterns of circles, lines, and zigzags on this old leather tapestry were made with **embossing tools**. Here the craftsman used premade stamps to create patterns. Note the gold leaf or gold paint added to certain areas.

TRANSFORMATION

WHAT DO YOU SEE?

MOMENT Autumn is my favorite time of the year. In New England, there is nothing more stunning than the color changes of the leaves. I picked up two leaves from the ground that seemed to be in the middle of that color change, brought the red, green, and yellow foliage home, and put them on my flatbed scanner. I find that it is compositionally better to make an arrangement of two rather than just using one object.

PHENOMENON I asked Michael Dosmann, curator at the Arnold Arboretum in Boston, to explain why leaves turn colors in autumn. He told me that the colors are caused by the breakdown of the green pigment called **chlorophyll**. Chlorophyll helps the leaves extract energy from sunlight. Since the chlorophyll is not being replenished in the autumn, the yellowish and red pigments now can be seen. The color changes are an example of autumn **pigment cycling**. Michael suggested the process is "an interesting dance—a subtraction, a reveal, and an addition!"

WHAT DO YOU SEE?

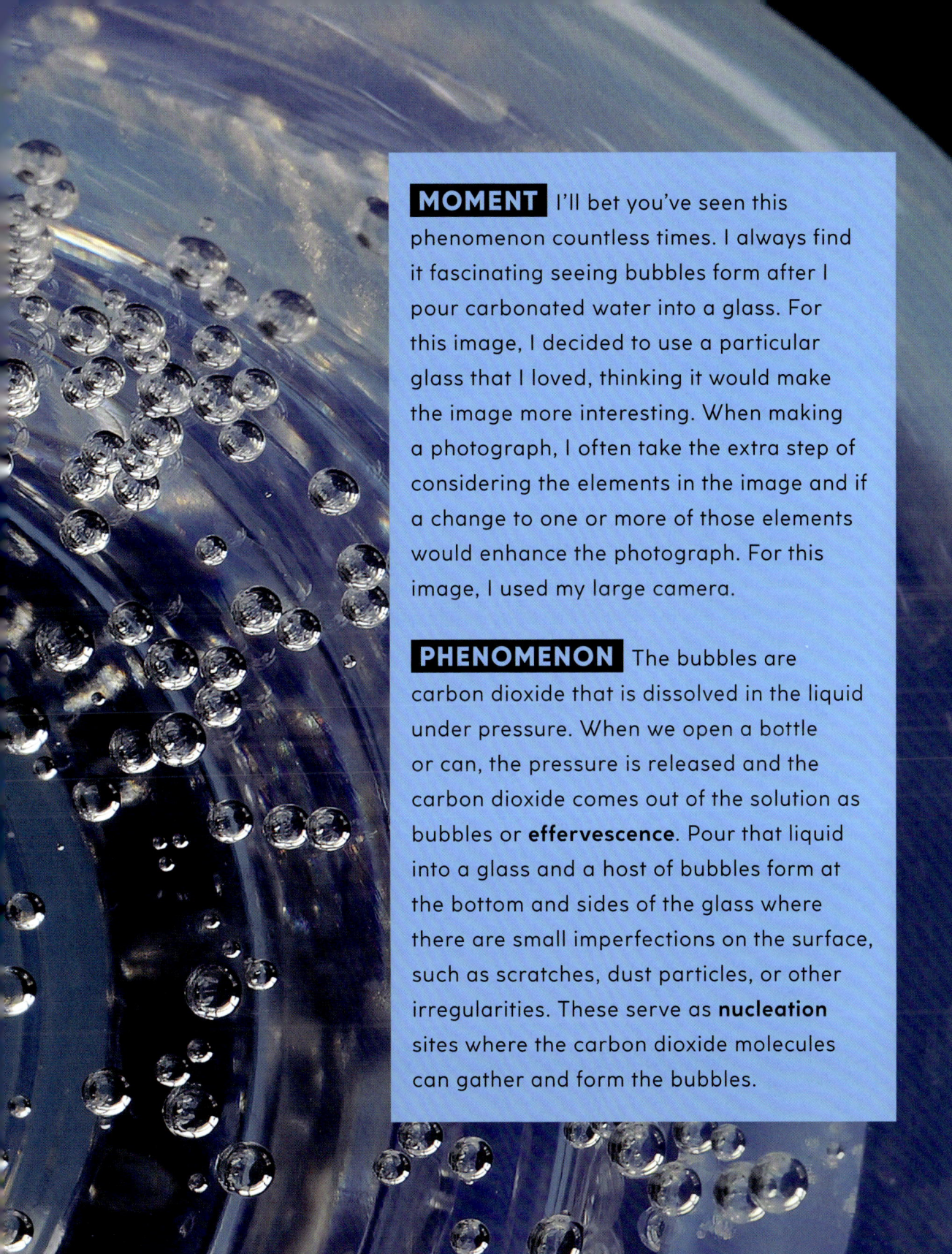

MOMENT I'll bet you've seen this phenomenon countless times. I always find it fascinating seeing bubbles form after I pour carbonated water into a glass. For this image, I decided to use a particular glass that I loved, thinking it would make the image more interesting. When making a photograph, I often take the extra step of considering the elements in the image and if a change to one or more of those elements would enhance the photograph. For this image, I used my large camera.

PHENOMENON The bubbles are carbon dioxide that is dissolved in the liquid under pressure. When we open a bottle or can, the pressure is released and the carbon dioxide comes out of the solution as bubbles or **effervescence**. Pour that liquid into a glass and a host of bubbles form at the bottom and sides of the glass where there are small imperfections on the surface, such as scratches, dust particles, or other irregularities. These serve as **nucleation** sites where the carbon dioxide molecules can gather and form the bubbles.

WHAT DO YOU SEE?

MOMENT Every morning, before I do anything else, I make a cup of coffee and sigh with happiness after taking my first gulp. This morning, I took a closer look than usual as the coffee was slowly pouring into the cup. I was fascinated with the movement of the bubbles going toward the sides of the cup. I quickly found my phone and made the image when the cup was full.

PHENOMENON The jet of liquid pouring from above creates bubbles from the **turbulent** flow of the coffee that traps air within the liquid. Any bubbles would disappear quickly in pure water, but they last longer in the coffee because it contains chemical ingredients that act a bit like soap molecules, coating a bubble's surface and making it more stable. At first, the larger bubbles form in the center, and they become smaller toward the perimeter. But if I let the coffee sit for a bit, the bubbles become more evenly sized, collect along the edge, and eventually disappear. Why? I'm not entirely sure, and neither are the scientist friends I've spoken to. There could be various things going on. Physicist Dan Harris suggested that it could be something called a **hydraulic jump**, which happens when there is an abrupt change in fluid depth, causing a fluid to flow outward. To answer why, I would need to do some serious experiments. That's how scientists try to figure out what matters and what doesn't. Otherwise, we're just guessing.

WHAT DO YOU SEE?

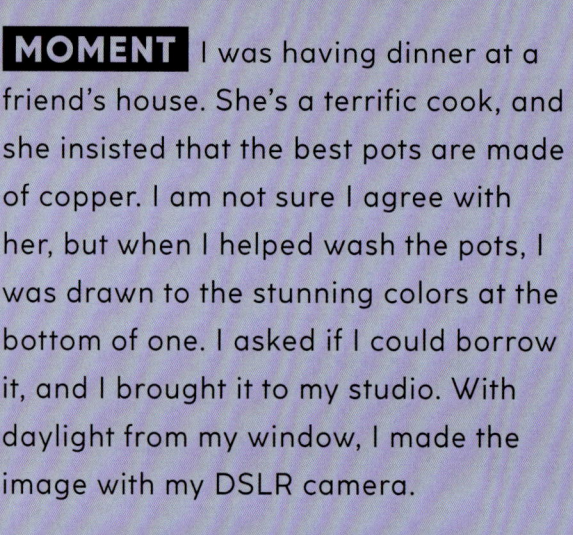

MOMENT I was having dinner at a friend's house. She's a terrific cook, and she insisted that the best pots are made of copper. I am not sure I agree with her, but when I helped wash the pots, I was drawn to the stunning colors at the bottom of one. I asked if I could borrow it, and I brought it to my studio. With daylight from my window, I made the image with my DSLR camera.

PHENOMENON When copper is exposed to heat and air, it undergoes **oxidation** (similar to what we saw on pages 76–77 with the rust on the metal fence), leading to the formation of a thin layer of copper compounds—especially copper carbonate—on its surface. We call the process **patina formation** (or just patination). Over time, different types of oxidation reactions take place, forming various copper compounds. The different compounds produce the colors.

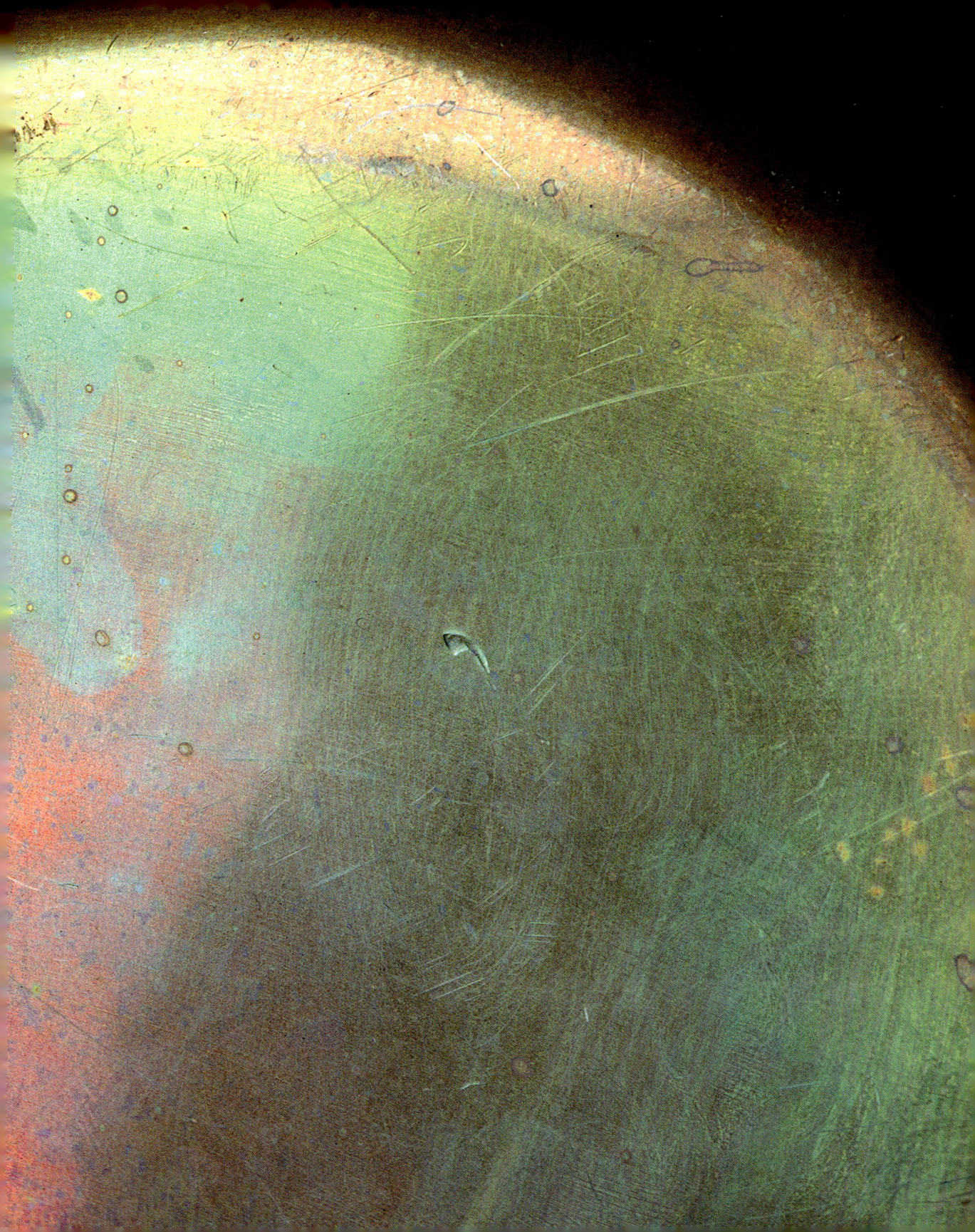

WHAT DO YOU SEE?

MOMENT While sautéing yellow, orange, red, and green peppers for a pasta dish on my induction stove, the glass cover on my pan began to reflect all the wonderful colors. I ran to get my phone to make the image. There are times when we have to act quickly in order to capture something that might never happen again or could be fleeting.

PHENOMENON Heat from the cooking surface caused the water from the peppers to vaporize, creating steam that was captured by the glass cover. The water **coalesced** into larger drops, forming **condensation** on the glass. The droplets act like lenses, transmitting the colors from the peppers onto the glass.

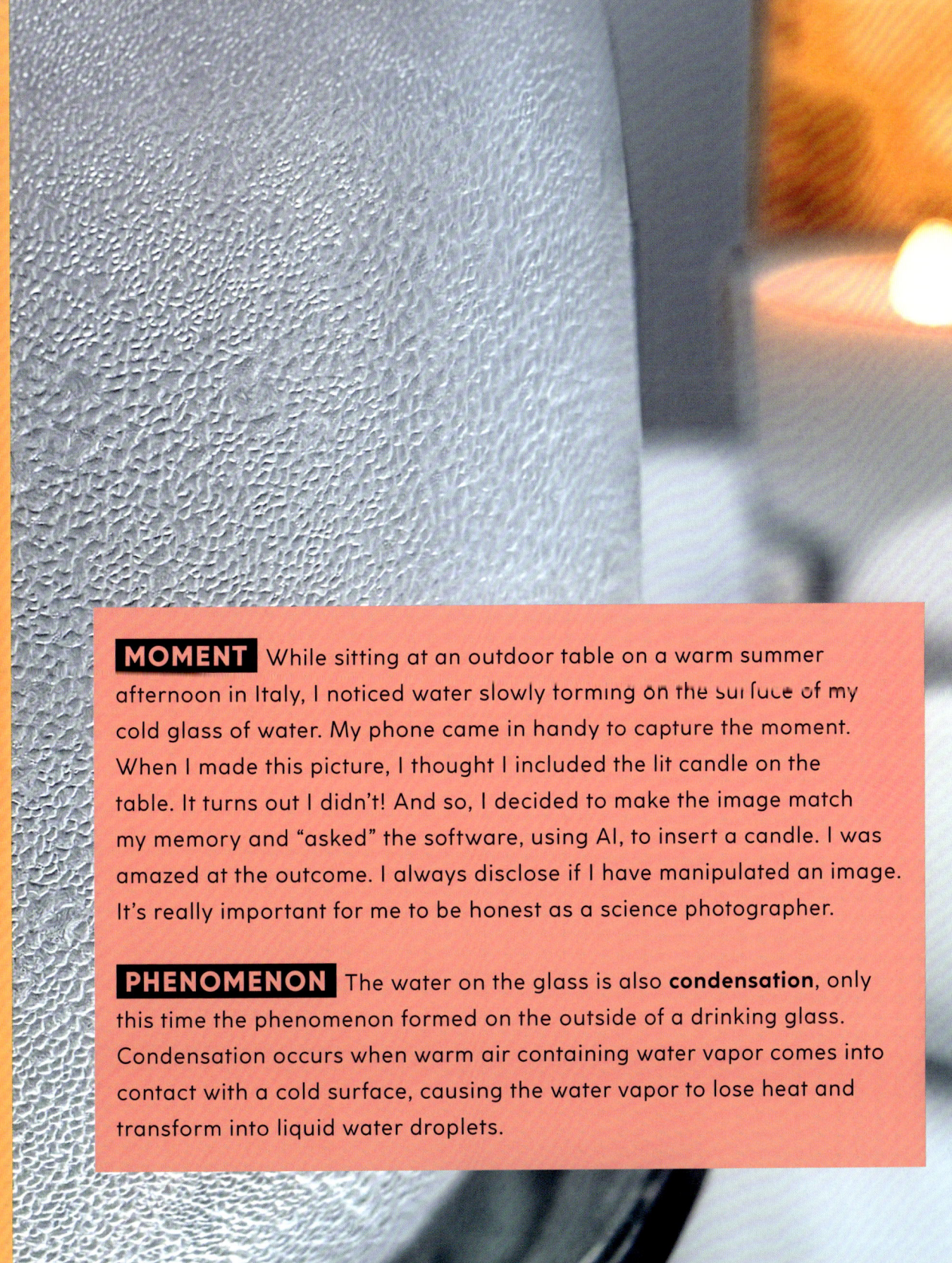

MOMENT While sitting at an outdoor table on a warm summer afternoon in Italy, I noticed water slowly forming on the surface of my cold glass of water. My phone came in handy to capture the moment. When I made this picture, I thought I included the lit candle on the table. It turns out I didn't! And so, I decided to make the image match my memory and "asked" the software, using AI, to insert a candle. I was amazed at the outcome. I always disclose if I have manipulated an image. It's really important for me to be honest as a science photographer.

PHENOMENON The water on the glass is also **condensation**, only this time the phenomenon formed on the outside of a drinking glass. Condensation occurs when warm air containing water vapor comes into contact with a cold surface, causing the water vapor to lose heat and transform into liquid water droplets.

SURFACES

WHAT DO YOU SEE?

MOMENT I often try to imagine how artists work with various materials. When I saw this scarf in the store, I thought it was quite beautiful. I was also curious about how the colors blended together. Making images is my way of seeing and better understanding why things are the way they are. Instead of using a camera to image the scarf, I used my scanner. I knew the scanner would be easier than trying to create the perfect setup with a camera and lighting. This time, the easier choice gave me the image I was hoping for.

PHENOMENON The artist who made this colorful scarf understood the phenomenon called **capillary action**. Capillary action, or wicking, is the flow of liquid to fill small spaces. An example of capillary action occurs when you put a straw in a drink and the liquid starts moving up the straw before you have even taken a sip. The narrower the straw, the more the surface of the liquid rises inside it. In this example of capillary action, **absorption** of the colored dyes causes the specifically placed dyes to "travel" on and within the fabric to create these amazing patterns. Note the areas where the dyes come to a full stop.

WHAT DO YOU SEE?

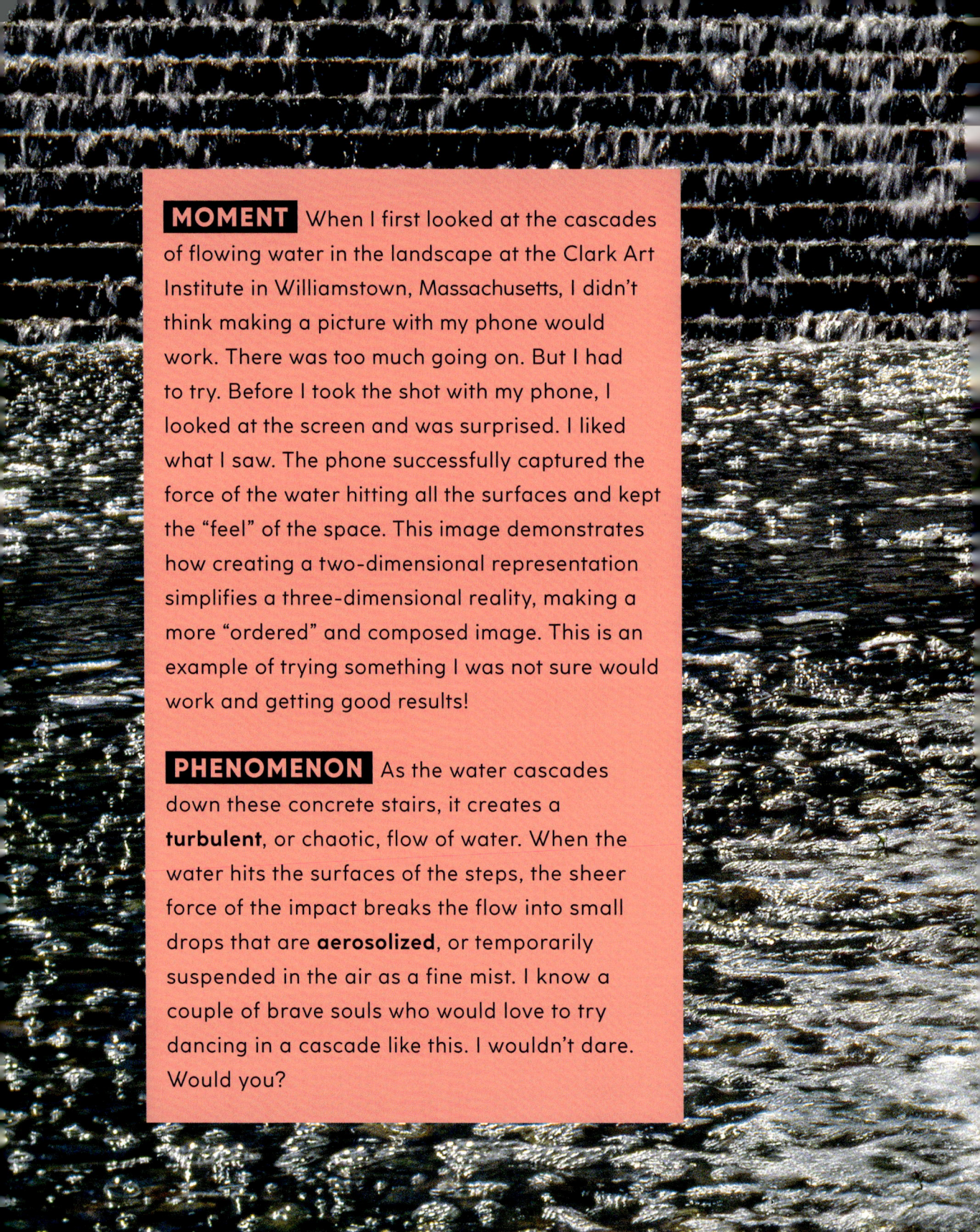

MOMENT When I first looked at the cascades of flowing water in the landscape at the Clark Art Institute in Williamstown, Massachusetts, I didn't think making a picture with my phone would work. There was too much going on. But I had to try. Before I took the shot with my phone, I looked at the screen and was surprised. I liked what I saw. The phone successfully captured the force of the water hitting all the surfaces and kept the "feel" of the space. This image demonstrates how creating a two-dimensional representation simplifies a three-dimensional reality, making a more "ordered" and composed image. This is an example of trying something I was not sure would work and getting good results!

PHENOMENON As the water cascades down these concrete stairs, it creates a **turbulent**, or chaotic, flow of water. When the water hits the surfaces of the steps, the sheer force of the impact breaks the flow into small drops that are **aerosolized**, or temporarily suspended in the air as a fine mist. I know a couple of brave souls who would love to try dancing in a cascade like this. I wouldn't dare. Would you?

WHAT DO YOU SEE?

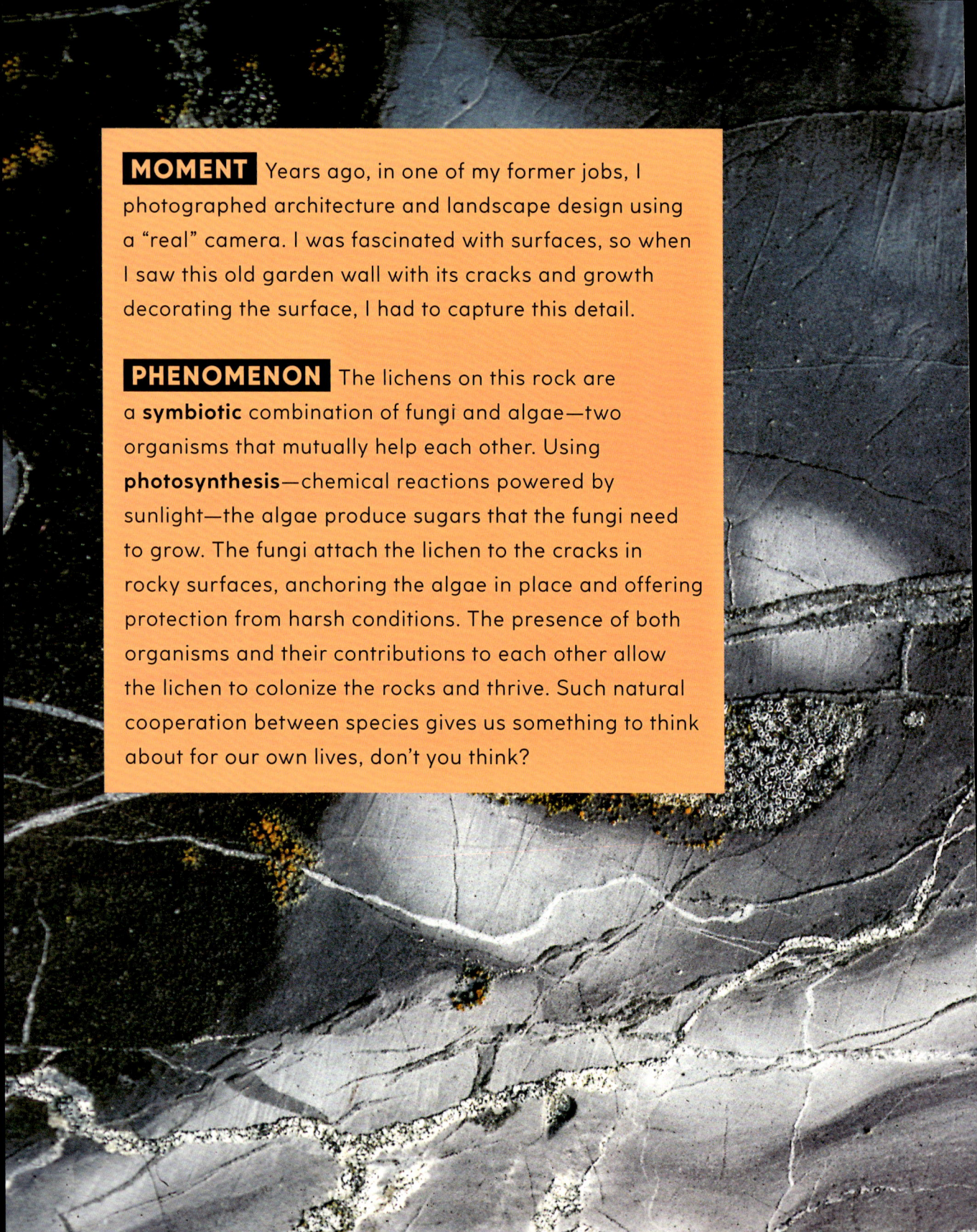

MOMENT Years ago, in one of my former jobs, I photographed architecture and landscape design using a "real" camera. I was fascinated with surfaces, so when I saw this old garden wall with its cracks and growth decorating the surface, I had to capture this detail.

PHENOMENON The lichens on this rock are a **symbiotic** combination of fungi and algae—two organisms that mutually help each other. Using **photosynthesis**—chemical reactions powered by sunlight—the algae produce sugars that the fungi need to grow. The fungi attach the lichen to the cracks in rocky surfaces, anchoring the algae in place and offering protection from harsh conditions. The presence of both organisms and their contributions to each other allow the lichen to colonize the rocks and thrive. Such natural cooperation between species gives us something to think about for our own lives, don't you think?

WHAT DO YOU SEE?

MOMENT As with many moments in this book, the moment that inspired this photograph was unplanned but indicative of how I look at the world and wonder about how what I see came to be. I was walking down the street when these three overlapping colors on the pavement caught my eye. I was curious about why the paint cracked the way that it did. I snapped the photo with my phone so that I could investigate the things I was wondering about. Besides being fascinated with what looked like cracking, I remember trying to figure out what order the colors were painted. Can you figure it out?

PHENOMENON I asked my friend Don Sadoway why the yellow paint appears to be **cracking** while the other colors are not. He wrote: "I wonder if yellow behaves as it does because its formulation (pigment + binder) is different from those of the other colors." Often, we can't be sure about why something is the way it is—although experiments can help us find out. For example, the pigments here could be chemically analyzed, and we could test how different paints dry on different types of surfaces.

WHAT DO YOU SEE?

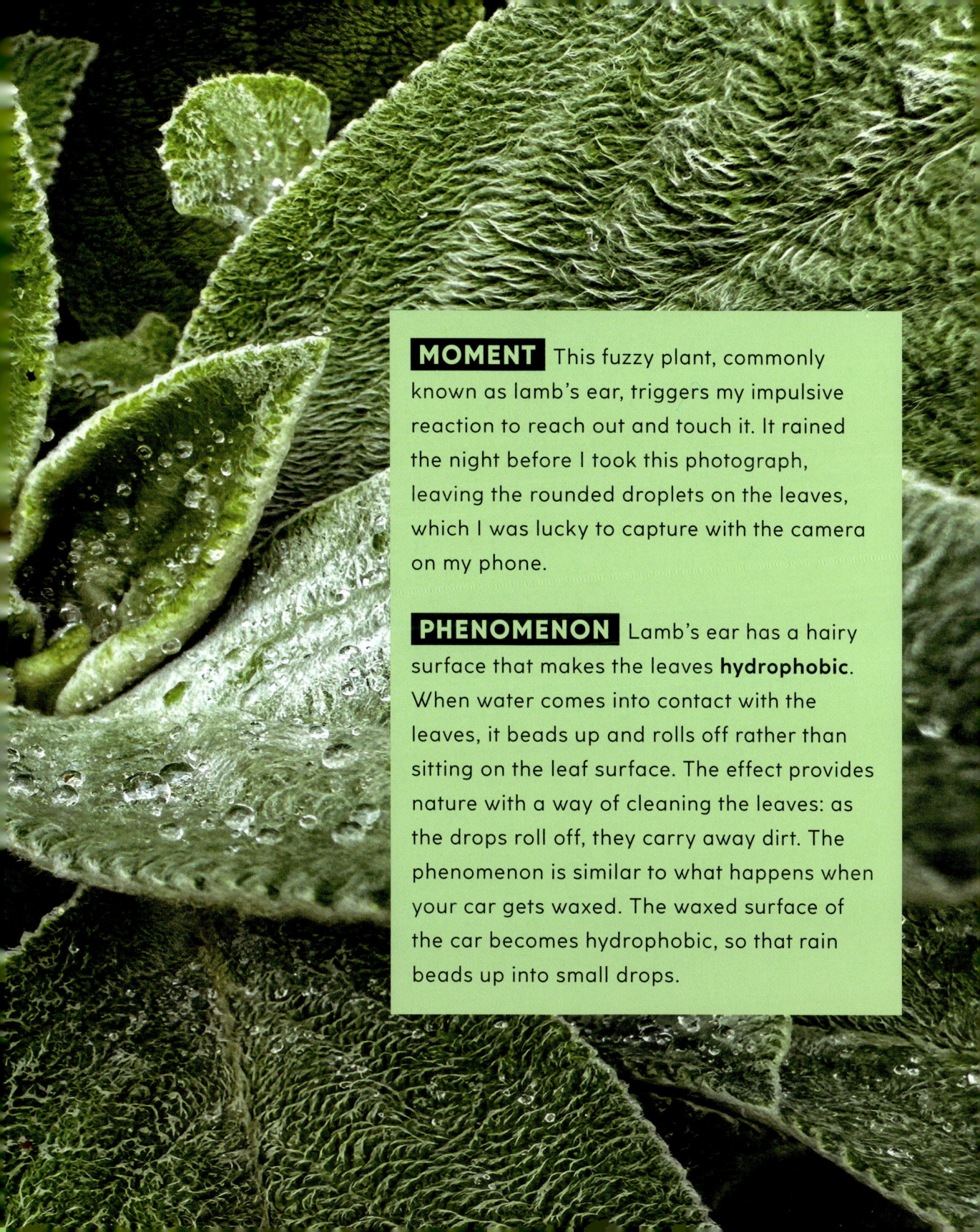

MOMENT This fuzzy plant, commonly known as lamb's ear, triggers my impulsive reaction to reach out and touch it. It rained the night before I took this photograph, leaving the rounded droplets on the leaves, which I was lucky to capture with the camera on my phone.

PHENOMENON Lamb's ear has a hairy surface that makes the leaves **hydrophobic**. When water comes into contact with the leaves, it beads up and rolls off rather than sitting on the leaf surface. The effect provides nature with a way of cleaning the leaves: as the drops roll off, they carry away dirt. The phenomenon is similar to what happens when your car gets waxed. The waxed surface of the car becomes hydrophobic, so that rain beads up into small drops.

WHAT DO YOU SEE?

MOMENT It's always fascinating to make visual connections between things that seem so far apart at first glance. At times, I make those connections after I make the images, as I did for this book. I remember photographing a section of a puddle while taking a walk after a rainfall. As usual, I took out my phone because I knew that I wanted to take a better look at the patterns later on. I remember thinking at the time that I had seen something like this before.

PHENOMENON The pollen grains in the water have layered themselves into **strata** as the wind pushed the small particles against each other. Watching these pollen particles move is similar to what some scientists do when they study **fluid dynamics**—the particles supply a visible trace of the patterns made by fluid flow.

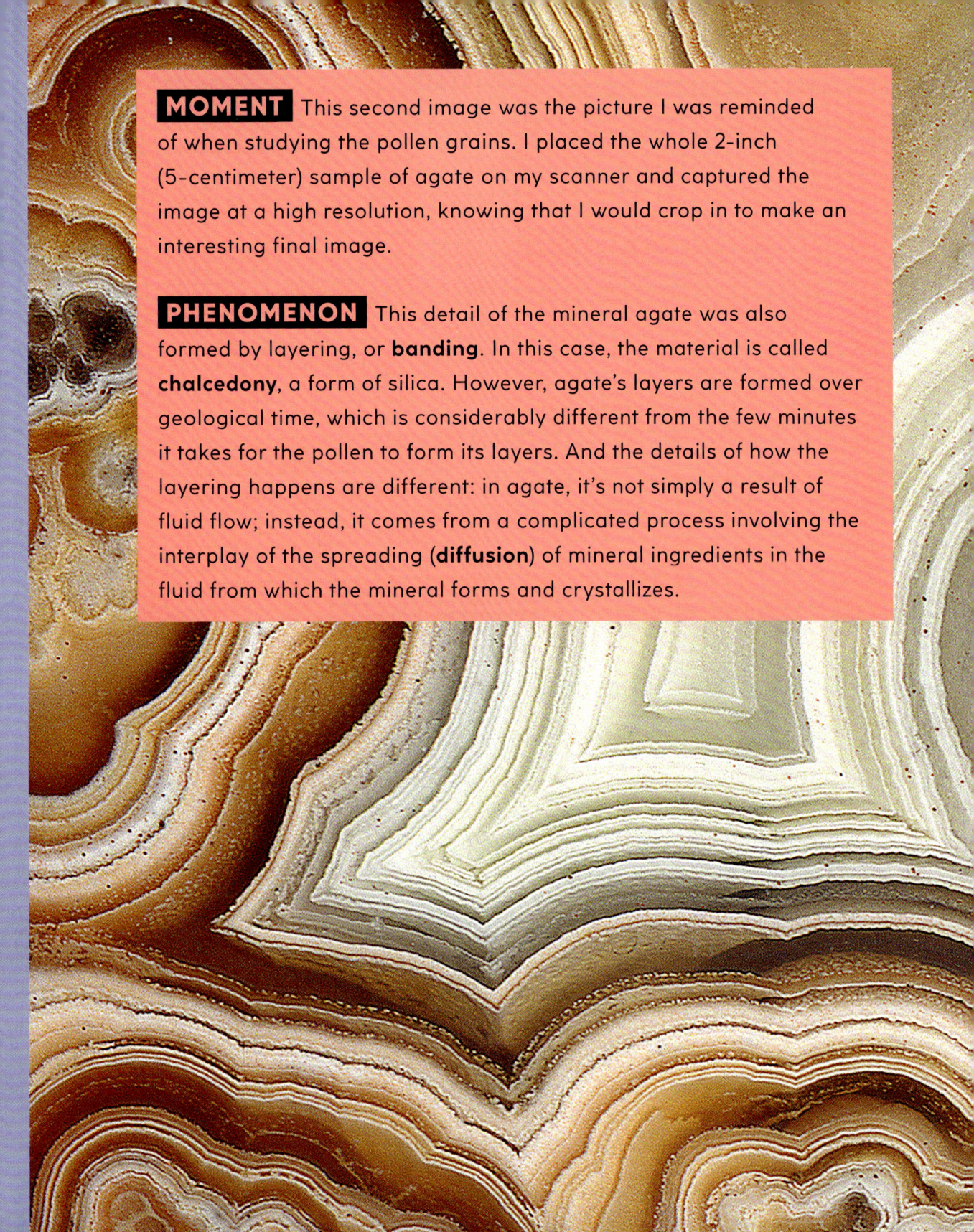

MOMENT This second image was the picture I was reminded of when studying the pollen grains. I placed the whole 2-inch (5-centimeter) sample of agate on my scanner and captured the image at a high resolution, knowing that I would crop in to make an interesting final image.

PHENOMENON This detail of the mineral agate was also formed by layering, or **banding**. In this case, the material is called **chalcedony**, a form of silica. However, agate's layers are formed over geological time, which is considerably different from the few minutes it takes for the pollen to form its layers. And the details of how the layering happens are different: in agate, it's not simply a result of fluid flow; instead, it comes from a complicated process involving the interplay of the spreading (**diffusion**) of mineral ingredients in the fluid from which the mineral forms and crystallizes.

ABOUT THE CHAPTER OPENERS

LIGHT AND SHADOW

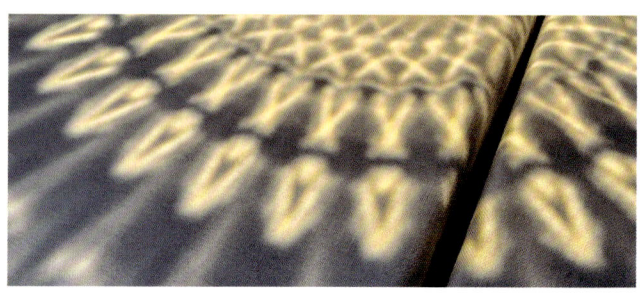

Refraction occurs when light travels from one transparent medium into a different transparent medium, changing the light's speed and bending its path. The bending of the light gives this cut-glass lamp a crystalline, diamond-like appearance when it passes through onto the tablecloth. The patterns that are cut into the glass create many different refracting surfaces at various angles, leading to complex light patterns. I will bet you have seen this elongation effect on your shadow when the sun is low and near the horizon.

FORM

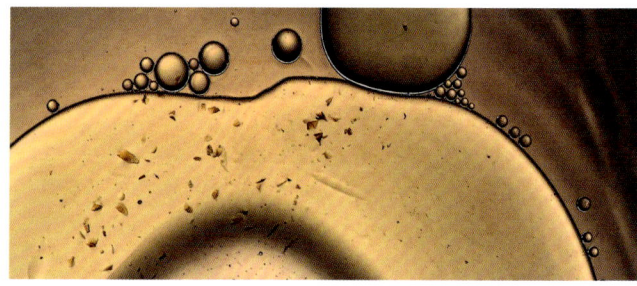

This photograph shows another example of immiscible liquids—oil and water. Oil is the larger circular form that takes up most of the image, and vinegar is the darker circular form at the top and right edge. Vinegar is largely water (in which some acetic acid is dissolved). Water molecules are **polar**—the negative electrons in the molecules are mostly at one end and positive electrons are at the other end. When water molecules are near each other, they mix easily since the negative ends are attracted to the positive ends of other molecules. We say that substances that dissolve easily in water, like acetic acid (which is also a polar molecule), are **hydrophilic**, or "water-loving." Oil molecules, on the other hand, are nonpolar (the negative electrons are evenly distributed throughout the oily hydrocarbon molecules). Oil doesn't mix with water because nonpolar molecules prefer to hang out with other nonpolar molecules, making oil **hydrophobic**, or "water-fearing."

TRACES

The artist who painted this wall probably didn't anticipate that Boston ivy would grow over the wonderful colors, or perhaps that was part of the plan. The vine climbs and adheres to the cement with holdfasts, which are tiny adhesive discs. The arrangement of leaves is **distichous**, meaning they alternate from one side to the other as they grow up the stem, which allows the vine to lie flat against the surface. Boston ivy is **deciduous**—it loses its leaves every year. The empty stems and the spaces between the leaves give us a sense of where leaves have fallen off—their traces.

TRANSFORMATION

This metal fence was originally painted green, but **corrosion** has caused the steel of the fence to rust and paint to flake off. Rust (iron oxide, which is red or yellowish) is formed from **oxidation**, the reaction of iron with oxygen and, in most cases, with water. Rust is extremely brittle and causes the surface of the metal to flake or powder. The paint can no longer stick to the rough surface, causing this mottled surface of many colors.

SURFACES

I took this picture on a clear, beautiful day because the **reflections** of these buildings reminded me of a tapestry. Imagine what the buildings look like that made this image. The wavy appearance of the buildings on water occurs because of the irregularities on the water's surface. If the water becomes more turbulent, the forms will be more broken up. Later, when the wind picked up, I stooped down to investigate the effect of both the camera angle and the more turbulent water on the image. The waves appeared exaggerated and the reflections were too distorted for my taste—not so much like a tapestry.

AND MY DEEPEST THANKS

Having family and friends giving constructive comments has always helped me in pretty much everything I do. Yosi Frankel, my grandson, who was sixteen at the time I put this book together, gave me incredibly important advice. I visited his science class, taught by their remarkable teacher William Mellman, to get their take on some of the images. They were painfully honest about a few they were not exactly crazy about, and I listened. Ellie, my granddaughter, gave valuable input as well. Science author Philip Ball contributed enormously, making sure I got the science right. I thank science writer David Chandler for his encouragement at the beginning of the project. My gratitude also goes to researchers Dan Harris, Christopher Baird, and Irmgard Bischofberger, who set me straight on a number of my perplexing questions about the science, and the remarkably talented editors and designers at MITeen Press, an imprint of Candlewick Press.

FELICE FRANKEL is a science photographer and author and a research scientist at the Massachusetts Institute of Technology in the department of chemical engineering with support from the departments of mechanical engineering and materials science and engineering. Her images have appeared in *Nature*, *Science*, *National Geographic*, and *Scientific American*, among other publications. Her book series The Visual Elements teaches visual communication to scientists and engineers. Felice Frankel is a Fellow of the American Association for the Advancement of Science and has been awarded a Guggenheim Fellowship and the Lennart Nilsson Award for scientific photography.

To all the curious

The MIT Press, the ☰MITeenPress colophon, and MITeen are trademarks of The MIT Press, a department of the Massachusetts Institute of Technology, and used under license from The MIT Press. The colophon and MITeen are registered in the US Patent and Trademark Office.

First edition 2025

Library of Congress Catalog Card Number pending
ISBN 978-1-5362-3489-3

25 26 27 28 29 30 CCP 10 9 8 7 6 5 4 3 2 1

Printed in Shenzhen, Guangdong, China

This book was typeset in CocoSharp.

MITeen Press
an imprint of Candlewick Press
99 Dover Street
Somerville, Massachusetts 02144

miteenpress.com
candlewick.com

EU Authorized Representative: HackettFlynn Ltd., 36 Cloch Choirneal, Balrothery, Co. Dublin, K32 C942, Ireland. EU@walkerpublishinggroup.com

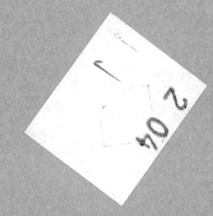